CHRISTMAS

SATB (with divisions) unaccompanied

OXFORD

Gaudete!

Annabel Rooney

MUSIC DEPARTMENT

OXFORD

UNIVERSITY PRESS

Gaudete!

Anon., *Piae Cantiones*, 1582

ANNABEL McLAUCHLAN ROONEY

¹ Rejoice! rejoice! Christ is born of the Virgin Mary; rejoice!

This piece has been recorded by the Choir of Christ's College, Cambridge, conducted by David Rowland, on the album *As a seed bursts forth* (Regent Records).

Duration: 2 mins

Printed in Great Britain

OXFORD UNIVERSITY PRESS, MUSIC DEPARTMENT, GREAT CLARENDON STREET, OXFORD OX2 6DP

Hoc quod op - ta - ba - mus; Car - mi - na lae - ti - ti - ae

De - vo - te red - da - mus.[2] Gau - de - te! gau - de - te!

37

Clau - sa per - tran - si - tur; Un - de Lux est or - ta, Sa - lus in -

Clau - sa per - tran - si - tur; Un - de Lux est or - ta, Sa - lus in -

Clau - sa per - tran - si - tur; Un - de Lux est or - ta, Sa - lus in -

Clau - sa per - tran - si - tur; Un - de Lux est or - ta, Sa - lus in -

42

-ve - ni - tur.[4] Gau - de - te! gau - de - te! Chris - tus est na - tus Ex Ma - ri - a

-ve - ni - tur.[4] Gau - de - te! gau - de - te! Chris - tus est na - tus Ex Ma - ri - a

-ve - ni - tur.[4] Gau - de - te! gau - de - te! Chris - tus est na - tus Ex Ma - ri - a

-ve - ni - tur.[4] Gau - de - te! gau - de - te! Chris - tus est na - tus Ex Ma - ri - a

[4] The closed gate of Ezekiel has been passed through;
from where the Light has risen [the East] salvation is found.

X821 **Gaudete!** ROONEY

[5] Therefore let our assembly sing praises now at this time of purification;
let it bless the Lord: greetings to our King.

ISBN 978-0-19-355173-2